BULLIED

by

Scott J. Langteau

illustrated by

Erik Ly

BULLIED

Published by Shake the Moon Books
www.shakethemoonbooks.com

ISBN ~ 978~0~692~14333~9
Copyright 2018 by Scott J. Langteau

Printed in China.

BULLIED does not attempt to address all targets of bullying,
their causes, effects, or solutions. It simply tries to tell one collection
of meaningful ~ and hopefully impactful experiences.

Special thanks to the following educators and administrators for their
invaluable insights and guidance on this title:
Chris Heagle, Karen Kercher, Chris Potter, and Corinne Zuleger

This book would not be possible without the loving support of Vi Truong.

Dedicated to
my younger self.

If I knew then what I know now,
I would never have been
so hard on myself.

Bullying:

When you repeatedly pick on someone because you think you're cooler, smarter, stronger or better than them.

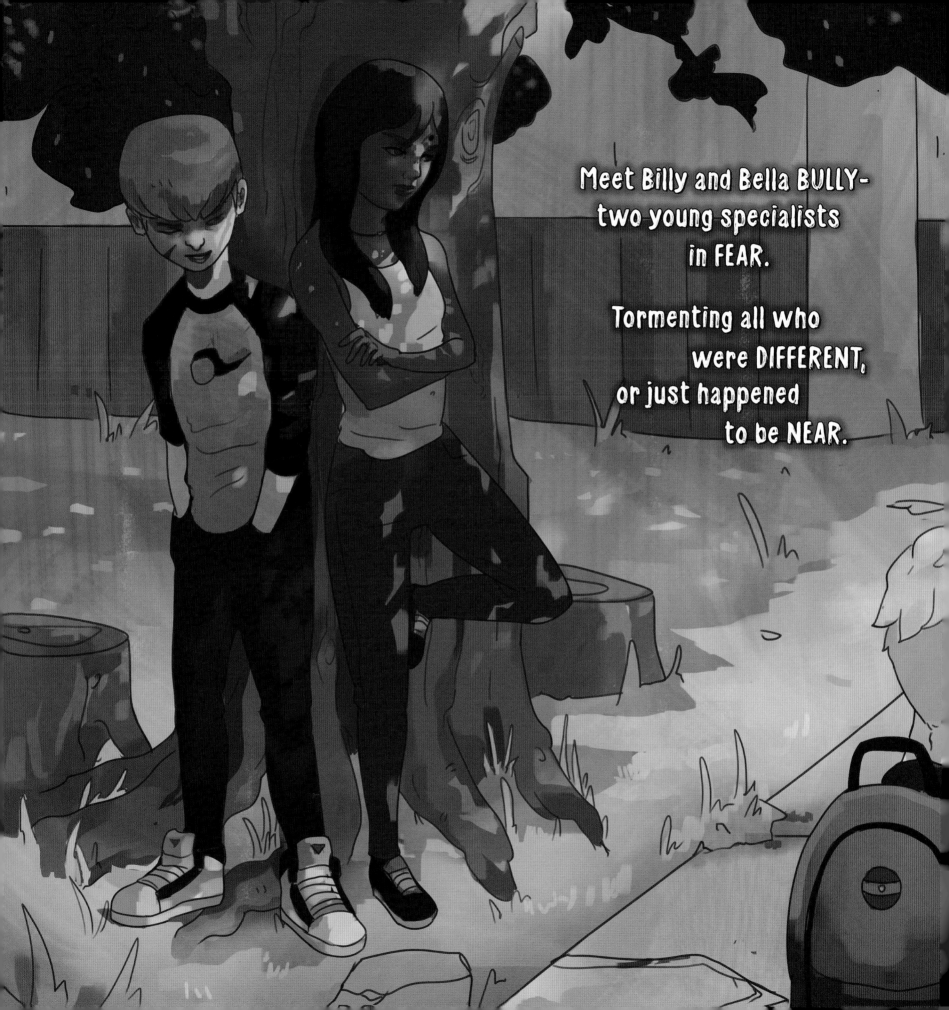

Bella STALKED her on the bus ride: "She's from that FOREIGN part of town."

Her TRADITIONS were not like THEIRS,

she wasn't SURE who she should BE.

Whenever parents
PHONED
the Bullies,
all THEIR parents
had to say –

was:

"Oh, those WIMPS
should TOUGHEN UP!
'Cause that's how
ALL
kids play
today!"

But that's a VERY WEAK excuse,
and what they CLAIM just isn't TRUE.

For there are
KIDS
as tough as
NAILS -

and some of THEM
don't make it through.

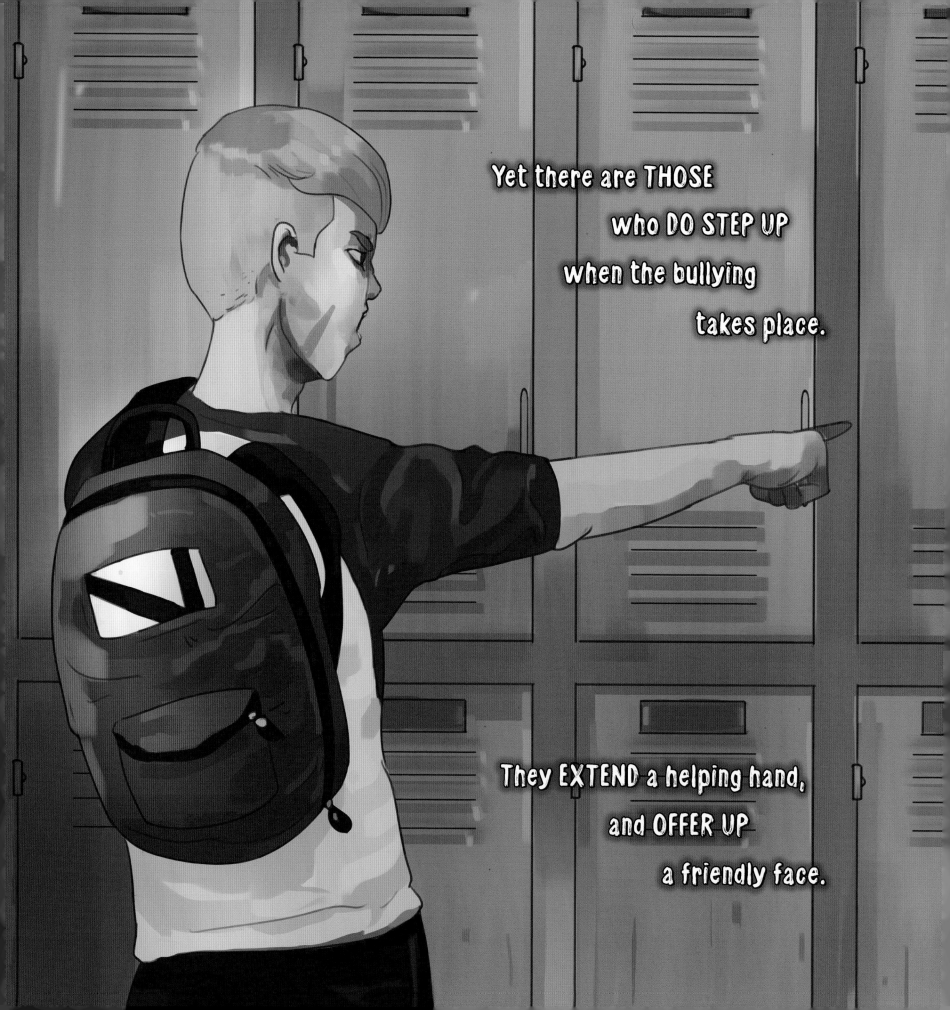

Though EVERY DAY proposed a CHALLENGE
to their HOPES and DREAMS and FEARS,
these kids had FAITH that life gets BETTER –
as DAYS turned quickly into YEARS.

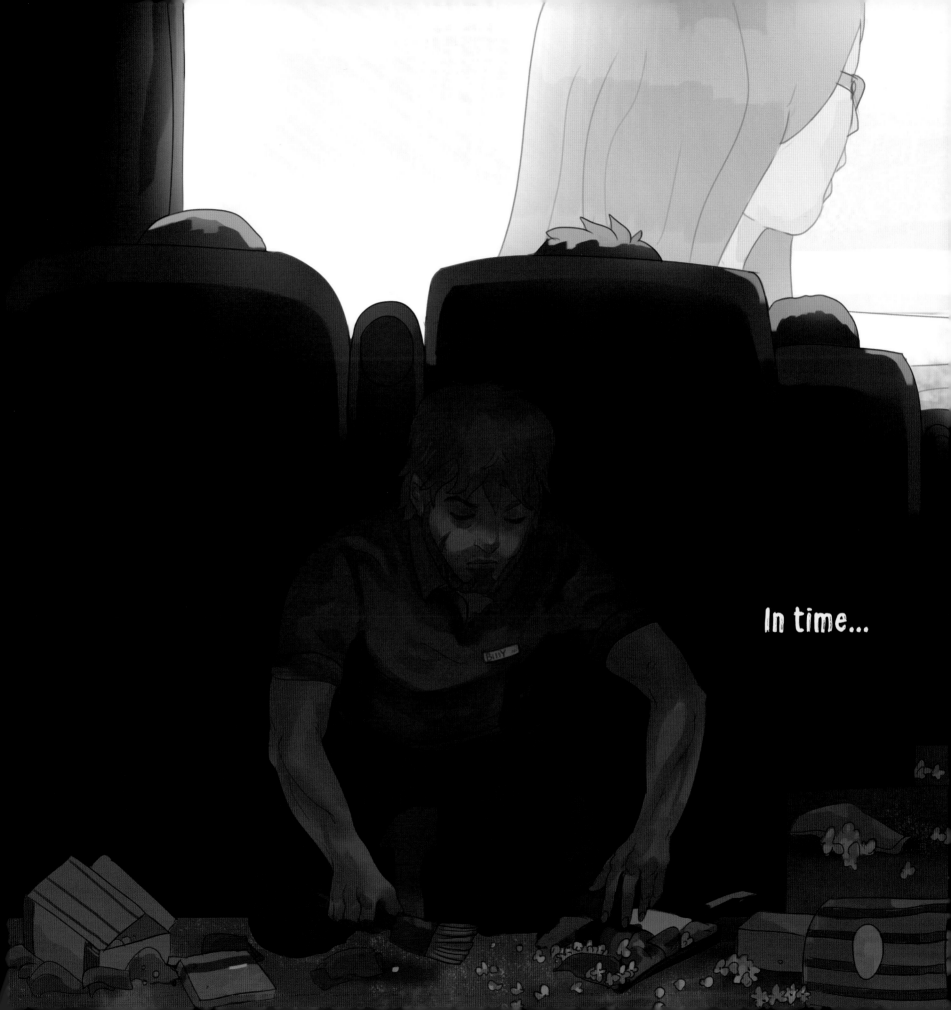

...our FANCY BOY became an ACTOR
    on both the BIG and LITTLE screen.
While BILLY sells the popcorn
    and SWEEPS THE FLOORS to keep them clean.

The NEW GIRL has now been ELECTED
to a POST with a whole lot of CLOUT!
And the LAWS on which she VOTES
have often HELPED our Bella out.

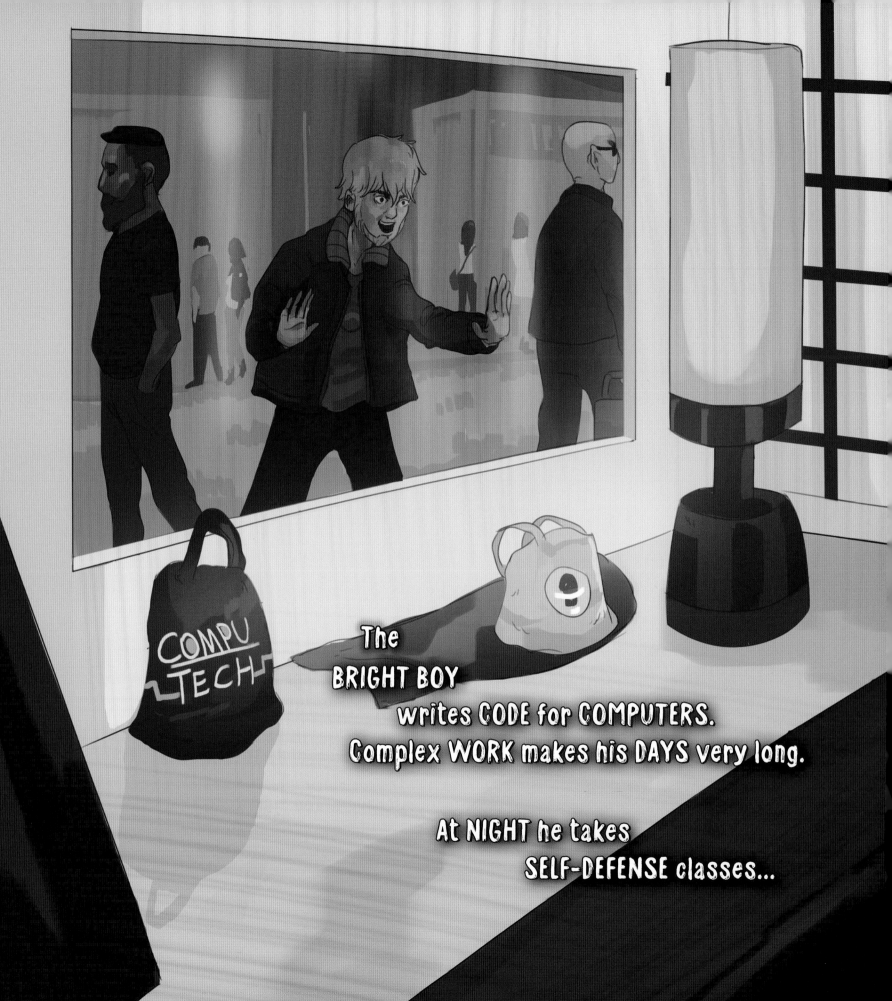

The
BRIGHT BOY
writes CODE for COMPUTERS.
Complex WORK makes his DAYS very long.

At NIGHT he takes
SELF-DEFENSE classes...

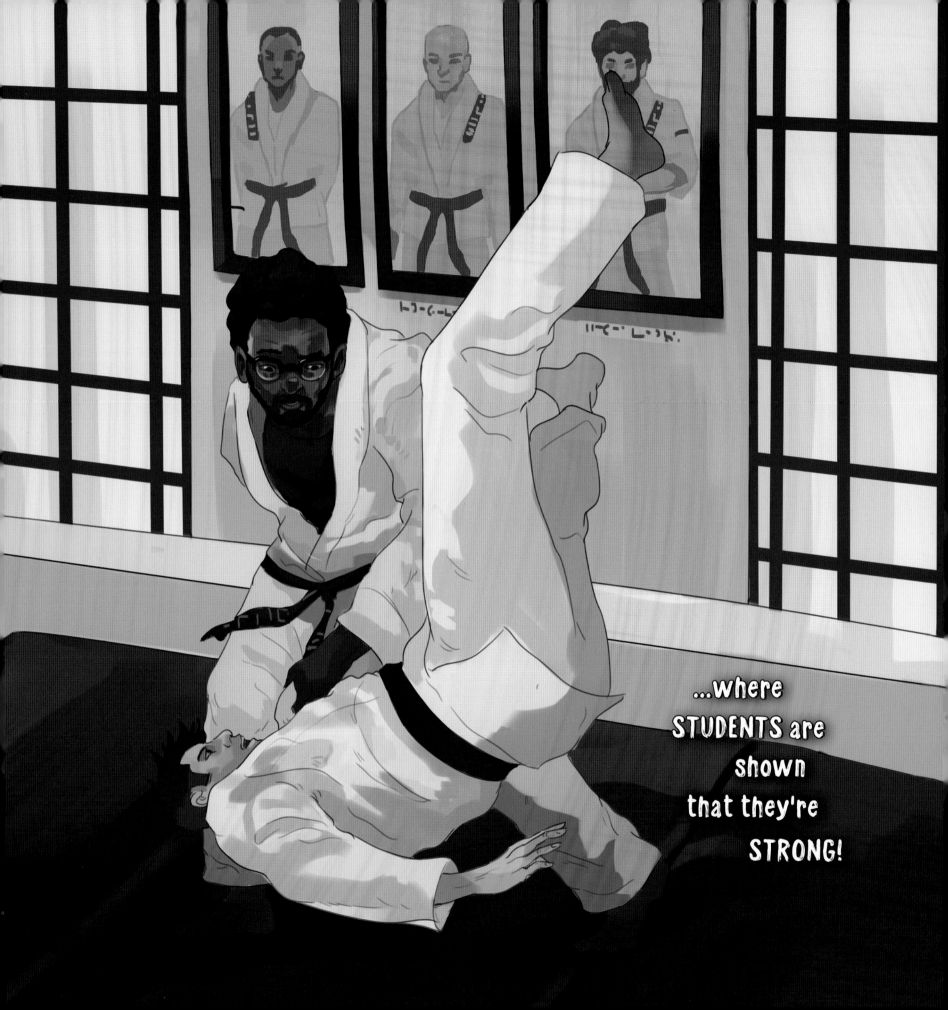

The quiet GHOST GIRL
took up writing –
CHILLING MYSTERIES she found
in her HEAD.

And though Bella once
set out to HAUNT her,
she now SHIVERS alone
in her BED!

The BULLIED kids? They never faltered.
Staying TRUE TO THEMSELVES paved the way.

As for BILLY and BELLA you ask?
What are THOSE TWO SOULS up to today?

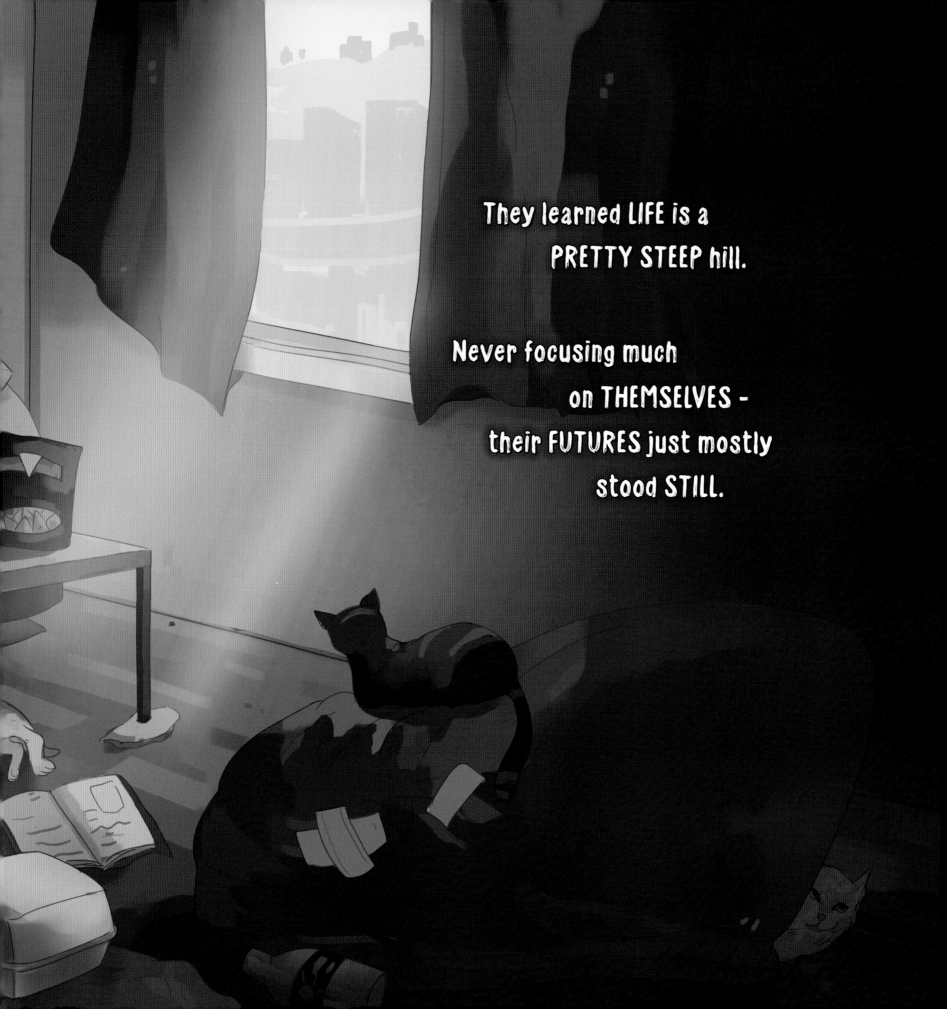

The TWO share a place where they LIVE,
and SOMETIMES, on the bus, now and then...

...they SILENTLY GAZE
out the window -
REFLECTING on what
might have BEEN.

Then TONIGHT,
    as they headed HOME,
        brushing PAST some kids in the PARK –

    a BEHAVIOR they saw left them SHAKEN,
        and their SHAME
            could have LIT UP the DARK!

'Cause it's NEVER TOO LATE to forge a new PATH...

Scott J. Langteau

Growing up in the small town of
Seymour Wisconsin, playtime came ready-made with Scott's 11
brothers and sisters. No lie! Having fun then meant grabbing a
sibling, heading outside and imagining a world around you.

That imagination brought Scott Theater degrees from the
University of Wisconsin ~ Stevens Point and Villanova University
before bringing him to L.A. where he's worked as a producer, writer
and actor for over 20 years. Best known for his work on the highly
acclaimed "Medal of Honor" & "Call of Duty" game franchises,
Scott has done work for companies including Disney, Pixar, DreamWorks, EA Games, and the Jim Henson Co..

Having experienced first-hand the lasting impact of many a bully's handiwork, the subject matter of BULLIED
is near to Scott's heart. To those dealing with these issues right now...seek out those who will help and
understand, believe in yourself, and know that what is happening to you is not your fault!
You too, will make it through!

Erik Ly

Erik Ly is a contemporary illustrator from Los Angeles, CA.

If he's not drawing or tabling at conventions, you can probably
catch him watching reruns of Seinfeld or creating yet another
playlist on iTunes.

He also loves sushi and has an unhealthy obsession with wasabi.

Also available from Shake the Moon Books

and author Scott J. Langteau

Sofa Boy (Ages 4-8)

A young boy discovers that lounging on his favorite sofa playing videogames around the clock is not all it's cracked up to be. His lack of attention to life's basics such as bathing, good food, fresh air, sunlight, and old fashioned exercise wreaks havoc on his young body, and before long our little lad finds himself a prisoner of his own designing, as well as the fascination of many an onlooker as he becomes literally joined at the hip with his increasingly disgusting environment. Sofa Boy is a funny and beautifully illustrated lesson-learned about moderation - a lesson that clearly speaks to all ages, and goes down easily with a warm and hearty chuckle.

The Question (Ages 4-8)

After watching the snowstorm of the season blow into his neighborhood, a young boy wakes to find his town literally buried beneath a mountain of snow. Possibly stuck inside his house for the rest of the winter, survival questions of every shape and size race through his mind - including one that tugs at his thoughts to the very end of his adventure. The Question is a wild journey through the mind of a child, with an ending so honestly relatable, you can't help but smile.

Shaking the Moon to Free the Stars...
(and other celestial observations).

Author Scott Langteau exposes and celebrates the "celestial joke that is life" through a hearty helping of humorous and often touching poetic observations creatively-penned and paired with hand-drawn sketches in an appealing style reminiscent of Shel Silverstein. These poems are designed to make you smile, smirk, cringe, ponder the nature of things, roll your eyes, call your mother, hug a child, kiss a dog, skip through the woods...and long for all sorts of life affirming and joyous things!

(Ages 13+)